CONTENTS

INTRODUCTION

The idea that the Great War marked a decisive step in the emancipation of women opening them the doors of the working world is deeply rooted in our collective memory. But were they satisfied before 1914 to stay at home and hold the house? The statistics compiled during the census of 1911 bring a whole different light to the subject and shows that women already represent more than 37% of the working population (38% in agricultural occupations, 35% in industry, 40% in commerce, 27% in administration and 83% in domestic service): more than seven million employees in total.

It Is true however, that these figures hide a very different reality. Many of them actually work at home. They participate in farm work in rural areas or perform sewing or laundry. In this second case, the salary depends on the number of items made and requires long hours of work. But, for the most part, women had to leave the house to go to the workplace. There are among other things more than two million workers (mainly in the textile sector), seven hundred thousand various employees (offices, post office, shops…) not forgetting the eight hundred thousand servants.

Nevertheless, whatever their situation, women remained subject to the guardianship of men (the husband at home, the boss at the factory or office). Since the second half of the nineteenth century, "Feminists" movements claimed a better recognition of women in society and called for greater gender equality. It must be remembered that for the same work, the women's salary was less than half than that of men's (a century later, this inequality is still relevant); remember also that they were absent from public debate and that the right to vote was systematically refused. While the Australians, Finnish, Norwegians and some others had already achieved this right, the big European powers remained hostile. The debate was bitter and agitated the societies of the time. In France, although proclaiming different arguments, right and left came together to say that women did not have a say in political life, even worse, asserted they did not have the capacity. For the right, historically conservative, the role of women must remain the one that's been hers for centuries, that of a stay-at-home mother; for the left, who believed that women were under the influence of the Church, claimed that granting this right to vote would directly threaten the balance of the Republic. With flawless determination, demonstrations and hardening of their actions – strong examples were of the suffragettes in Britain – left us to think that the claims were close to bearing their first fruits in the of year 1914. But mobilisation turned everything upside down. When war broke out, it's a whole nation that rallied to the sacred Union called by the President of the Republic, Raymond Poincaré. As with the political parties, the Church and the pacifists movements, women also put to one side their struggle and devote themselves to defending their country. "A strange impulse brought people together, in a fraternity that has never been reviewed. No more political factions, no more enemy castes: quarrels were forgotten and disunited hands sought to embrace each other." (*Bleu Horizon - Pages de la Grande Guerre*, Roland Dorgelès). Women, too, went to war…

✦ Activist meeting in favour of the suffragettes, Paris 1908.
gallica.bnf.fr/agence Rol.

WOMEN AND THE MOBILISATION

THE SEPARATION

If the collective memory has retained the patriotic drive on which propaganda has carefully put the accent, for the mobilisation of the August 1914, the departure of the men was the first drama of the war. Mobilisation marked a turning point just as sudden as brutal in the lives of couples. Nearly three million men left their family and work. The usual way of life during peacetime was abandoned. "In the space of a week, the village had completely changed, there was no longer a single man between 20 and 30 years old, they were all at war." (*Une soupe aux herbes sauvages*, Emilie Carles).

✦ Man sobbing in the arms of his wife and child before leaving, Gare de l'Est, Paris, August 1914.
Bridgeman images © Jacques Moreau.

✦ Anonymous lithograph, *The departure of the soldier*, Germany. The Historial de la Grande Guerre in Peronne © Yazid Medmoun.

By giving up their homes, the men left the women alone, to fend for themselves. Those who until then, had no other career or other perspectives became by the strength of things support and head of the family. An effective separation that leads to the redistribution of tasks. From afar, through correspondence, the men tried to continue to exercise their role. They provided advice to their wives for sowing, harvesting, on the household accounts: "I wonder if you managed to get rid of the beets; the sowing, you can do after." (Anonymous letter, September 1916).

Faced with the upheaval engendered by this separation, the State legislates throughout the conflict: allocation to the women of the mobilised marriage by power of attorney, authorisation for married women to exercise paternal authority...

✦ Photographs of German, French and British couples. The photograph taken before the departure with their wife and sometimes children, was carried by the soldier and treasured in the pocket of their uniform. The sight of their beloved ones was a precious comfort when nostalgia or sadness seizes him.
The Historial de la Grande Guerre in Peronne © Yazid Medmoun.

War broke out while in the countryside people prepared for the harvest. In a France still largely rural, they must organise urgently if they were not to lose the crops, indispensable to feed the country. From 6 August, René Viviani, President of the Council, appeals to the women, inviting them to take part in the war efforts, just like their husbands gone to the Front: "Stand up, French women [...]! Replace in the field of work those who are in the field of battle. Get ready to show them cultivated land tomorrow, harvests collected, fields seeded. There is not in these difficult times a lesser labour; everything is great that serves the country. Stand, take action, and toil! Tomorrow there will be glory for everyone."

In the same way, an appeal is made to qualified nurses to provide assistance to the injured: "Mme Messimy, wife of the War Minister, organised in Paris an ambulance where she would gladly welcome the nurses with a diploma from Red Cross societies and who had not taken up a position." (*Le Matin*, 3 August 1914).

The war was no longer just a men's affair, society as a whole mobilised.

✦ Poster "Aux femmes françaises!" (To french Women) signed René Viviani, 6 August 1914.
The Historial de la Grande Guerre in Peronne © Yazid Medmoun.

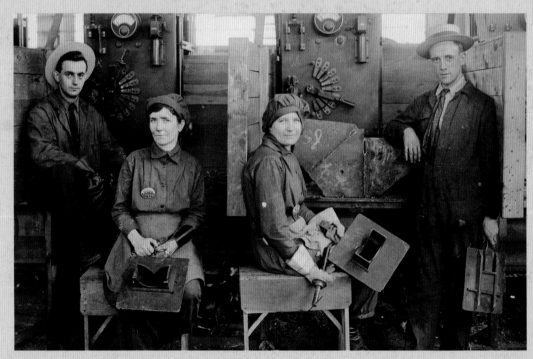

✦ Welders, Hog Island Shipyard, 1918, photograph by Paul Thompson. The U.S. National Archives and Records Administration.

✦ Poster "For Every fighter a woman worker" by Ernest Hamlin Baker, United States, 1918. In all belligerent countries, women were called to mobilise. The United States did not break the rule when they entered the war in 1917. This poster echoes the call of René Viviani and echoes in its own way the famous slogan "Replace in the field of work those who are in the field of battle": walking in tight ranks, tools worn like a rifle, uniform-looking outfits... is reinforced by the second part of the slogan which evokes a second line of defense. The Historial de la Grande Guerre in Peronne © Yazid Medmoun.

WOMEN AND THE WAR EFFORTS

THE FARM WOMEN

Aux Cultivatrices
femmes de Mobilisés qui par leur
Energie et leur Labeur ont assuré le
RAVITAILLEMENT de la FRANCE
la Société d'Agriculture de l'Arrondissement de MAYENNE
décerne un Diplôme d'honneur
à Madame Quentin aimable, à la Baulière St de Gennes

Mayenne, le 11 novembre 1918
Le Secrétaire,   Le Président.

✦ Certificate awarded to Mrs. Quentin Aimable on 11 November "To the women farmers of mobilised men who through their energy and their labour assured the supplies of France". The Historial de la Grande Guerre in Peronne © Yazid Medmoun.

In addition to the usual daily tasks, it was up to women to cultivate the land. But in the month of August 1914, the certainty that the war would only last a few weeks, a few months at most, still led people believing that the duration would be brief. With the stabilisation of the Front, more than eight hundred and fifty thousand women who, beyond that first harvest, must manage the farms over the long term. Pauline Lombard recalls: "To replace the men gone to war, my mother would often go to help her family in the fields. We walked the ten kilometers that separated her home village of Hébécourt, from the south of Amiens. There, I would find my cousins. This work allowed us to live a little better too because during these four years, my mother received half of the salary of my father." (Family Archives).

It was exhausting work that fell on the women, a job for which they are not necessarily prepared, and all the more painful as most tools are not adapted to their size. "Before leaving, [my brother] Joseph had me learned to plough. The hard part was not so much to fend for myself with a mule or a team of cows but to hold the handle of the plough. I was not tall. I remember that we had a simple plough, a plough with a handle made for a man. For me, it was far too high. When I was doing a furrow with this equipment, every time I hit a stone, I received the handle in the chest or in the face. For me, plowing was a real Calvary." (*Une soupe aux herbes sauvages*, Emilie Carles).

✦ "Les champs près du front" (fields near the Front), 1916, Maurice Le Poitevin, 329th French Infantry regiment.
The Historial de la Grande Guerre in Peronne © Yazid Medmoun.

✦ Woman harvesting a field in the Beauce, *Le monde illustré*, 2 September 1916.
The Historial de la Grande Guerre in Peronne.

✦ Poster, "They serve France, how can I serve Canada?" This poster by the Canadian government invites the public, notably women, to economically participate in the war efforts by buying Victory Bonds. In a skillful way, this subscription was presented as modest gesture in comparison to the colossal efforts provided by French women in the fields. It should be noted that the illustration of the poster copies exactly a photograph of Jean-Baptiste Tournassoud, of the photographic unit in the French army.
The Historial de la Grande Guerre in Peronne © Yazid Medmoun.

✦ A shell worker, Citroën factory, Quai Javel, Paris, 1915.
BDIC, Fonds Valois.

THE FACTORY WORKERS

In 1906, female enrollment was 1% in metallurgy (maintenance and cleaning), 12% in the chemical industry, 36% in the textile industry and 90% in the confection. The Great War did not mark the entrance of women in industry. But the departure of almost three million men in August 1914 followed by three other millions before the summer of 1915, resulted in a 20% drop in the male labour force and, as a result, a sharp slowdown in production, even the closure of factories and workshops. Nearly two millions of non-mobilised people are thus unemployed in October 1914. Yet the need for arms and ammunition continued to grow. A war industry running at full speed proved indispensable and it was vital to revive the economic activity by adapting it to the military needs. Specialised workers recalled from the Front did not provide the necessary manpower, and so the workshops opened up to women. For those who lived in uncertainty, it was the opportunity to perceive a salary to subsist (the allowance of 1.50 francs per day, supplemented by 0.50 francs per child under 16 years was insufficient). Industries needed to modernise their production tools to adapt to this new workforce.

✦ Cartoon by Albert Guillaume: "FROM TIC TO TAC: — Madam, I give you my eight days... I'm hired in an explosives factory... — Oh Well! My girl, if you drop as many things there as here... you will not be there for long!...", *Le Pays de France*, 3 August 1916.

For some, this was the opportunity to hire unskilled labour to be assigned to repetitive tasks and to be underpaid, although the salary of the ammunition workers was double the amount collected by women in their traditional sectors of work. Others, like André Citroën, strived to provide better working conditions and to respond to the specific needs of his workers (nurseries, nursing rooms...).

Ten hour days, toxic fumes, corrosive chemical product and noise made the work gruelling. The journalist Marcelle Capy, hired to do an article, testifies: "The worker, constantly standing, grasps the shell, by the opening on the device.

The munition in place, she lowers it, checks the dimensions (this is the purpose of the operation), then takes the shell and moves it to the left. Each shell weighs seven kilos. In normal production time, 2,500 shells pass through her hands over an eleven hour day. As she has to lift each shell twice, she carries 35,000 kg in one day. After three quarters of an hour, I confessed myself defeated." The arrival of this female workforce coincides, it is true, with the Taylorisation of the work that imposed sustained rhythm. In addition, the use of picric acid caused diseases and the yellowing of the skin and hair, workers received the nickname of "canaries": "[...] the wife of Juvenet spoke out severely about the other wives of soldiers on leave. I who had met soldiers of all colours, I thought at first that she was a Hindu, although her skin seemed to me more saffron than copper. Mrs. Juvenet had already guessed the cause of the marital recession:
— Didn't you know that I was working in the ammunition?
— Yes, but why did you get dyed yellow?
— It's melinite, she explained." (*Mémoire d'un rat*, Pierre Chain).

As Marcelle Capy says, you have to "be hungry to do this job", and many people were hungry in 1917, although the situation was less dramatic than Germany where famine had hit hard. The "munitionnettes" (female ammunition workers) – follow suit with the ten thousand "midinettes" (female textile industry workers) – who protested against the rise in prices and went on strike to claim an increase in wages, the allocation for mobilised woman (normally not cumulative to an active salary) and the English week (rest on Saturday afternoon and Sunday). At first these movements were not taken seriously as Joguenard's comment shows in an article of the newspaper *Sur le Vif*, on 2 June: "It was a strike that everyone, except the great couturiers, found charming, they cheered for a few days in our streets and boulevards creating a slight diversion from our concerns and our sadness."

General Joseph Joffre already noted in 1915 that "if women working in the factories stopped for twenty minutes, the Allies would lose the war". A possible paralysis of the industry could not be considered. Joined by some male sectors, the strikers gained satisfaction and the English week was granted under the law of 11 June 1917.

✦The "Midinettes" strikes in Paris, *Sur le Vif*, 2 June 1917.
The Historial de la Grande Guerre in Peronne.

✦ Cartoon, "THE COUTURE IS SHAKEN: Listen... it's really is not possible for me to lengthen wages, I can shorten the skirts by twenty centimetres. That would give you less work to do." *Le Pays de France*, 13 April 1916.

In early 1918, at the height of their hiring, not to mention the thousands of women who made equipment items for the army from home, there were four hundred and thirty thousand "munitionnettes", around one-quarter of the war's labour force.

As a first step, the priority of the State was to attribute the vacant places in administration to a family member of a soldier; besides the urgent need for personnel, the goal was to reassure the soldier in guaranteeing him to return to his position once the war ended. But this measure alone did not enable all the vacant positions to be filled. At the postal offices – eleven thousand women (sorting, lettering, telegraphists...) replaced the mobilised men. In August 1914, although the Union transport had always opposed it, the Seine Prefet authorised the hiring of women to ensure continuity of service. They become conductors then drivers of trams and their numbers grew from two thousand six hundred in 1915 to nearly six thousand in 1916.

✦ Female chimney sweep on the roves of Paris, November 1917.
© Excelsior. l'Equipe / Roger-Viollet.

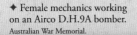

✦ Female mechanics working on an Airco D.H.9A bomber.
Australian War Memorial.

✦ "German women in times of war", *Revue hebdomadaire de guerre illustrée*, Berlin drawing by Kate Holff.
The Historial de la Grande Guerre in Peronne © Yazid Medmoun.

Although the unions ensured that "the employment of women constitutes a serious danger for the working class", women were gradually exercising almost all trades until now reserved for men: gas employees, mechanics, chimney sweeps, railways switchers, delivery men, longshoremen, firemen, newspaper salesmen, rangers and others were replaced in the public services by women, things that were now essential to the country's economic activity.

✦ Post-girls, *La Guerre documentée*, No.44.
The Historial de la Grande Guerre in Peronne.

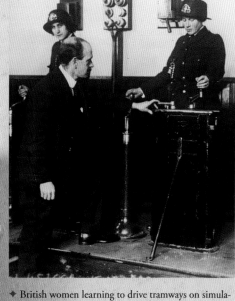

✦ British women learning to drive tramways on simulators. gallica.bnf.fr / Agence Rol.

CHARITIES

Very quickly, associations, foundations and charities organised themselves to ward off the emergency. The majority of these organisations were led by women of the upper middle class who found here the opportunity to assert just as much as for their sense of social responsibilities for that of their patriotic commitment. "[...] we were at the beginning of winter. Patriotic leagues had appealed to the heart of French women. Mothers, sisters, fiances, wives, mistresses of the soldiers and the old maids, all the women knitted. The men's bags were filled with warm items, woollen socks, gloves, mittens, choker, scarves, balaclavas, flannel belts, sweaters, knitwear [...]." (*La Main coupée*, Blaise Cendrars).

These actions of the charities had intended to provide assistance to soldiers on the front by sending parcels containing everything that could relieve them in their daily lives (food, clothes...) or during their convalescence at the rear: "An extremely interesting work, The Home of the Wounded, Assistance to the Wounded Military, was founded under the patronage of Public Assistance, with the aim of providing wounded soldiers treated in the hospitals of Paris all the material and moral support necessary to ease their suffering, to console them, and to distract them as much as possible." (*L'Anti-Boche illustré*, 20 February 1915).

✦ Canister in the Serbian Day colours, 25 June 1916.
The Historial de la Grande Guerre in Peronne © Yazid Medmoun.

They also tried to support civilians struggling to sustain themselves, the orphans and widows of war, and refugees who had fled Belgium and Northern France in face of the German invasion. Many volunteers welcomed thus poor women, often isolated, and offered them in exchange for minor work (knitting, sewing...) a modest retribution.

Along with these charities, many donation appeals were launched during special days: Serbian day, day of the "Poilus" (French soldiers) or orphans of war... Poster campaigns or quests conducted in the streets called for solidarity, generosity and the population's patriotic spirit.

✦ Examples of knitting patterns in *La Mode*, No.11, 14 March 1915. The Historial de la Grande Guerre in Peronne.

✦ Everywhere people work to help the defenders of the patriotic land fight against the cold. In this photograph we see numerous workers of the Festa sewing rooms in Beausoleil. This work room sent over five hundred articles every week to the front, *Excelsior*, 17 november 1914.
The Historial de la Grande Guerre in Peronne.

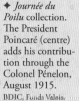

✦ *Journée du Poilu* collection. The President Poincaré (centre) adds his contribution through the Colonel Pénelon, August 1915.
BDIC, Fonda Valoin

✦ Poster for the *Journée du Poilu* (French soldier day), 25 and 26 December 1915. The Historial de la Grande Guerre in Peronne © Yazid Medmoun.

✦ Pressed paper badges sold during the Journée du Poilu, 1915. The Historial de la Grande Guerre in Peronne © Yazid Medmoun.

ANNE MORGAN (1873-1952)

Daughter of a wealthy American banker, Anne Morgan was convinced that women had a role to play in society and invested at a very young age in charities in the USA. She did not take long to assert herself as a pioneer of humanitarian actions during wartime. From 1914, she raised funds to help the French war wounded. In April 1917, she moved to Blérancourt, in the Aisne, and created with her friend Anne Murray Dike the "Comité Américain pour les Régions Dévastées" (CARD) – American Committee for Devastated Regions, in order to help the civilian population particularly affected by the destruction and the lack in food supplies. Dispensaries were created for this population, shops, libraries, schools and nurseries. Beyond the material help the aim was to provide moral support indispensable in the restoration of social life. After making them operational, she entrusted these structures to French women she had previously trained in social actions. From 1917 to 1924, the actions of Anne Morgan touched almost sixty thousand people in one hundred and twenty-seven municipalities of the region. She was awarded the Legion of Honour in 1924 before being raised to the rank of Commander of the Legion of Honour in 1932. She continued her actions during the Second World War.

✦ Anne Morgan (left) and her friend Anne Murray Dike, 1915.
Wikimedia Commons.

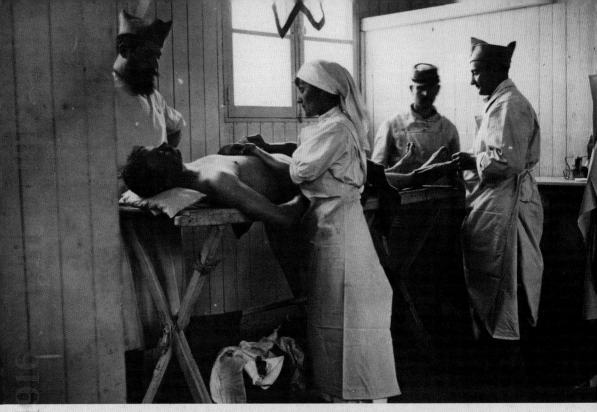

✦ Nurse assisting the surgeon in the operations room. The Historial de la Grande Guerre in Peronne © Yazid Medmoun.

WOMEN AND SUPPORT FOR SOLDIERS

THE NURSES

No armed forces anticipated the carnage of the first weeks of war and, on the French side, there were no military hospitals near the Northern or Eastern borders. Health services could only rely on doctors and nurses attached to the different units and were quickly overwhelmed. At the end of 1914, confronted with the sanitary drama, several companies of the Red Cross (the relief society for the wounded military, French Women's Union and The French Ladies Association), set up rural hospitals along the Front Line and auxiliary hospitals at the rear. In the December 1915 bulletin, the french Women's Union proudly announced that hospital facilities had thus grown from 10,043 beds during the mobilisation to 27,080 in September 1915. This network was completed by volunteer hospitals installed in their own properties by women from the aristocracy or the upper middle class.

✦ Patriotic plate "Women of France 1916".
The Historial de la Grande Guerre in Peronne © Yazid Medmoun.

The staff of the Red Cross, that already counted thousands of members before the beginning of the hostilities, were reinforced by nuns, graduate nurses and auxiliaries who received accelerated training. Most being volunteers (seventy thousand out of the hundred and ten thousand French nurses, more than 63%, in 1918), there were few or no women looking for a salary for subsistence as in the war industry. Most of them were women and young girls from affluent backgrounds who had received an education to prepare them for marriage, maternity and keeping the house. "[...] now that they are alone, all, even those the most accustomed to a life of leisure, women young or old and girls offer with admirable momentum their services to the Relief Societies for the wounded. The headquarters of the three companies of the Red Cross was literally invaded. [...] all women driven by a great surge of patriotism and self-denial wanted to be nurses." (*Souvenirs d'une infirmière*, Julie Crémieux).

While providing precious help to the wounded, they find in their new functions the opportunity to escape a time of tradition and to be otherwise accomplished.

The nurses accomplish many tasks: toilet of the wounded, care, administration of necessary treatments, help during meal times, assistance to doctors and surgeons during operations ... More importantly, the "Les anges blancs" (white angels) provide moral support to the wounded who felt for them admiration and gratitude.

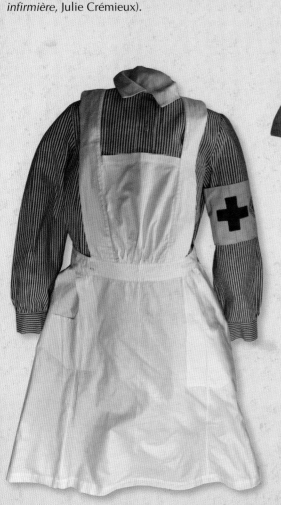

✦ German nurse's uniform.
The Historial de la Grande Guerre in Peronne © Yazid Medmoun.

✦ Australian nurse's uniform.
Franco-Australian Museum in Villers-Bretonneux.

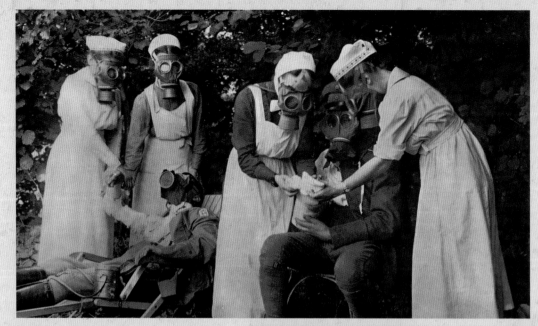

✦ German nurses wearing gas masks, censored photography by Paul Hoffman.
The Historial de la Grande Guerre in Peronne © Yazid Medmoun.

Throughout the journey to the hospital, the admission to convalescence, this female presence was the comfort of which those who, coming out of hell from the trenches, had been deprived: "Why then are there no women here, when they die? Oh! These male nurses, who circulate with their big shoes, their big hands, their big voices, their big pipes, who do not know how to undress them, who do not know how to wash them, who do not know how to change the position of their pillow, who do not know how to talk to them, who do not know to smile, who do not know how to put a hand on their forehead where sweat sticks to the hair, or the ear close to their lips when they call mother, who ignores what's going on right there!" (*La Sainte Face*, Elie Faure).

Faced with the suffering of men, the most horrific wounds, exhausted by long days of work, nurses – officiating for many near the Front – were sometimes themselves exposed directly to danger. Several hundred were thus victims of bombings, gas or diseases contracted during their service but also of depression.

✦ Maire Curie at the wheel of one of the radiological vans, 1917.
Wikimedia Commons.

MARIE CURIE (1867-1934)

Determined to put the fruit her research to the service of her adopted country, Marie Curie overcame administrative and military reluctance to constitute a radiology department. Eighteen vehicles "Les petites Curie" (the little curies) moved close to the Front Line. Thanks to X-rays, the surgeons located precisely where the bullets and shrapnel were in the bruised bodies, allowed them to detect fractures and

✦ X-ray of a wounded soldier hit in the chest by a bullet that can be clearly seen in the X-ray. The Historial de la Grande Guerre in Peronne © Yazid Medmoun.

avoid amputation or the death of many wounded. More than a million soldiers thus benefited from the assistance of radiology during the conflict. Paradox for one that who saved so many lives, Marie Curie succumbed to Aplastic anemia, probably related to prolonged exposure to radium.

WARTIME GODMOTHERS

In the face of a war that was bogged down and dragged on, the morale of men was at its lowest. Correspondence was the only way to maintain the link with the family. In France, nearly five million letters transited each day between the rear and the Front. The arrival of the mail was eagerly awaited by all. For families, it was above all a deep relief: the husband, the son or brother was alive. For fighters, this was the possibility to forget the war for a few moments and indulge themselves with their loved ones.
"I keep my wife's letters, said Blaire.
— Me, I send them back to her.
— I keep them. Here they are.
Eudore exhibits a pack of used papers, shiny, whose darkness modestly obscures darkness.
— I keep them. Sometimes I read them again. When we are cold and hurt, I read them again. It does not warm you up, but it's not far off." (*Le Feu, journal d'une escouade*, Henri Barbusse).

Conversely, for isolated soldiers – without family or originating from invaded areas under enemy control –, the lack of correspondence was cruel and gave rise to a momentum of compassion at the rear. A first charity, "La famille d'un soldat" (*The family of a soldier)*, was created in Angers in January 1915 by Marguerite de Lens; it called for women to devote themselves to these soldiers. From this appeal, a reader of the newspaper *La Croix* answers: "It's a long time now that I hesitate

✦ British post-girls sorting the military post, 1918. gallica.bnf.fr / Agence Rol.

✦ Photograph sent by a Wartime godmother to her 'godson', she writes: "Mélanie Joffre to her godson of the Great War 1914". The Historial de la Grande Guerre in Peronne © Yazid Medmoun.

BREVET de MARRAINE

Je Soussigné:
avoir eu pour Marraine de guerre
M

✦ Wartime godmother certificate; this one is issued directly by the 'godson' in recognition of the benefactor.
The Historial de la Grande Guerre in Peronne © Yazid Medmoun.

to become a wartime godmother, thinking that whoever gets me would not be favoured. Think, a farmer... with my husband on the Front Line and three children, who is used to writing only since war broke out, tells you that it will not be exempt of spelling errors. But I am moved by your call, if you believe that a good heart, a little religion and some packages will be enough, send a name recommended by his chaplain, I will do my best". The role of these wartime godmothers was to maintain an epistolary link with these men and to bring them moral and emotional support that they lacked. And it's in this setting alone that godmothers of all ages and from all conditions conceived their role.

What at first was meant to be a patriotic action among others took, in a few month an unexpected magnitude. When the 4 December 1915, the magazine *La Vie parisienne* opened its columns to the requesting fighters, it published only two adverts; one year later, three full pages are devoted to it and the magazine informed its readers that "given the overabundance of requests, a delay of four weeks from the date of receipt of the advert and the date of their publication".

✦ Postcard, "The Norwegian pot of War godmothers".
The Historial de la Grande Guerre in Peronne © Yazid Medmoun.

Soon, the action is no longer limited to a simple 'patriotic' correspondence and turns into epistolary flirtation. The terms 'young', 'pretty' and 'sentimental' that we find in many adverts were, as such, revealing: "Young doctor wants flirtation with a spiritual and coquettish correspondence", "Officer Aviator 26 years old, wants pretty wartime godmother, spir., feels., susceptible get to know each other during leave". (adverts published in *La Vie parisienne*, 1916).

The wartime godmother sees her image suffer and became synonymous with light and frivolous women, denounced by part of civil society as responsible for the decay of the good mores, and by the army who fears to find enemy spies. For these whistle-blowers, the godmother was a threat to social order, and the most vindictive do not hesitate to talk about 'prostitution agencies'. Despite the controversies, these relationships continue, experience various fortunes, sometimes ending with a wedding …

✦ Humorist postcard: "letter from an unknown wartime godmother — THE SENDER: Godmother, you are, I am certain, sweet smelling like a rose, as thin and lively as a leprechaun and as beautiful as a flower!... — THE RECEIVER: Oh, how the description suits!...".
The Historial de la Grande Guerre in Peronne © Yazid Medmoun.

PROSTITUTION

In August 1914, the army did not take into account the problem related to the separation of couples since the war was to be short lived. The question of emotional suffering and, of course, sexual needs did not arise, all the more that war was presented as purifying and moralising. As the months went by, this frustration nevertheless became a strong reality: "[...] the thought of flesh haunts the dugouts. I do not need for proof the engravings of *La Vie parisienne* which repeatedly decorate the shuttering boards. [...] the blonde with big eyes and voluptuous whiteness who, languidly, stretches out in her chair to my right, reminds me that beyond the lines, life continues; [...] and just two hundred kilometers away, there are human creatures that taste all the joys of a refined civilization." (*Carnets d'un fantassin*, Charles Delvert).

"I have to tell you, my little spring flower, that I adore you more than ever, in the evening "ma petite gogosse", I think I'm with you and sometimes I have dreams that are deceiving and the next day I'm all wet my darling, when can I get drunk from your kisses, your crazy caresses, I hope soon. That day, I will swoon you on the bed, under my crazy kisses." (Letter from a soldier to his wife, 30 January 1917, cited in *La Première Guerre mondiale – L'éclatement d'un monde,* Jay Murray Winter).

To break this distance, women try to join their husbands in the quarters at the rear. But the army strictly controls access to the army zone and forbids wives access. Only a safe-conduct in proper terms allowed these women to clandestinely find their husbands and to pass discreetly, sometimes through kindness of a compassionate officer – a few hours with him would do. As the safe-conduct opposite shows, the motive justifying the request sometimes leaves us perplexed...

✦ Zouave laying next to a sculpture in the sand of his wife, Oost-Dunkerke-Bains, Balgium, June 1915. BDIC, Fonds Valois.

✦ Front cover of *La Vie parisienne*, 12 June 1916, "A taste... who is not at the front! (for those that are)". BDIC, Fonds Valois.

✦ A *Sauf-Conduit* issued to Jeanne Thomas and valid from 19 November to 18 December 1915. At the top of the document is the motive for her having to go to Baudricourt in the Artois. not far from where her husband's regiment was stationed on this date. by passing through Amiens and Abbeville: "To collect her child and take him back to Paris". But this motive, if credible is to be taken with caution. For, on this date her son Eugene, aged 4 years is in a boarding school in Levallois-Perret, in the Paris region... Family archives.

Paradoxically, in the face of its incapacity to curb prostitution, while at the same time refusing the legitimate wives, the army decides after having forbidden it, to tolerate it: "The good morale of the soldier before good morals!" Houses of Tolerance multiply in cities located near the Front, where the demand was the strongest, but also near the major railway stations at the rear, the terminus for soldiers on leave.

✦ Box containing tubes of cream to prevent sexually transmittable diseases.
The Historial de la Grande Guerre in Peronne © Yazid Medmoun.

The army even ended up, to control it better, to organise prostitution and a circular of the 13 March 1918 by General Mordacq, signed by Clemenceau in person, confirmed the creation of the famous BMC, the "*Bordels Militaires de Campagne*" (Country military brothels). "I have the honour to address you herewith a copy of a letter from the Lieutenant-Colonel Congdon and a letter from Captain Maude asking me to intervene with you to receive permission to organise in Amiens a house of tolerance exclusively for officers. This house could be installed in a neighborhood near the train station, without any sign outside to attract attention, so as to avoid all scandal [...] and to reinforce the precautions taken for public health by submitting the women of this house to frequent sanitary visits". (Letter from the commander to the mayor of Amiens, 28 September 1917, Departmental Archives of the Somme).

of the wife became the nightmare of the fighter, absent from the home: "Women stood... you see them in the suburbs with working men, men that earn and who do not respect the home... women, they could not live with twenty-five pennies a day and ten pennies per child... So, it's with the men's factory money that they feed their families..." (*Clavel chez les majors*, Leon Werth).

These BMCs were subject to military regulations; the hygiene rules were strict and prostitutes were followed by a doctor to stem transmission of venereal disease. A soldier from the 128th division reported in September 1917: "Just three hundred metres from my divisional training camp in Champagne, existed the *Cabaret des six fesses* (The six buttocks cabaret), a cottage in the woods that sold drinks... and other things too, where soldiers were often reported to have a venereal disease". (*Les Soldats de la Grande Guerre*, Jacques Meyer).

Parallel to this professional prostitution, occasional prostitution was developing, women plagued by poverty who in it found an ultimate livelihood. The infidelity

✦ A French soldier and a prostitute pose in front of a Brothel in Paris, Photograph by Eugène Atget.
Los Angeles County Museum of Art.

✦ Prices for a brothel for German Soldiers, distinctively stating the consummation of "extras".
The Historial de la Grande Guerre in Peronne © Yazid Medmoun.

ARMY THEATRE

Separated from their families, prey to the depression, the fighters feel the urge to entertain in the encampments and find themselves on impromptu stages singing or performing. Photographs that immortalised these improvised productions clearly show how much the absence of women weighed on the men and some do not hesitate to disguise themselves to bring a female presence to the troop.

If the army, anxious to maintain military discipline, was reluctant to offer entertainment to men, it was resolute, in the face of the imperious necessity to maintain the morale of the troops. On the initiative of Émile Fabre, director of the French Comedy, and Alphonse Séché, journalist, writer and director of theatre, the "Théâtre aux armées" (Army Theatre) was founded in 1916. Financed by funds collected at the rear, performances, strictly supervised by the military authorities, were provided by professional entertainers. It was the opportunity for actresses to participate, in their own way, to the war efforts.

The first performance took place in minimalist conditions on 9 February 1916 in Le Crocq, a small village of the Somme, a few kilometres from the Front. Progressively, the materials improved and mobile stages follow the actors. In total, there were close to two million soldiers that attended these shows.

✦ Two soldiers disguised in civilian clothes, Cappy, Somme, 5 October 1916. BDIC, Fonds Valois.

SARAH BERNHARDT (1844-1923)

Although amputated above the right knee in February 1915, Sarah Bernhardt was vigorously engaged in the war despite the fact she could only move around in a wheelchair. She mainly performed for the neutral countries to enhance the French culture, critiicised by the Germans. In September 1916, she left for an eighteen-month tour of the United States to convince them to go to war. She also took an active part in the "Théâtre aux armées" and participated in many representations closer to the fighters and the Front, which she visited several times. Her performances were concluded by a vibrant call to arms and by the singing of "La Marseillaise". She wrote several patriotic plays and movies, including a play entitled "Cathedrals", where the latter were gifted with words, she played the role of the Strasbourg Cathedral!

✦ Sarah Bernhardt on stage in London, *L'Image de la guerre*, February 1916. In the play "The theatre of the field of honour", Sarah plays the role of a young soldier that dies on the battlefield after being covered with glory. Her last play mirrors her own engagement: "Do not pardon them, for they know what they are doing". The Historial de la Grande Guerre in Peronne.

WOMEN AND THE ENEMY

COHABITATION

In the first weeks of war, the German troops invaded Luxembourg, Belgium then the north of France, pushing thousands of civilians to exodus. Others choose to stay at home and prepare to live under the Occupation. The first contact was brutal. As in any invasion, women were often the first victims of war and rapes were common.

Faced with the need by the occupiers to restore calm, these outbreaks became quickly scarce and life returned to some form of normality. They would have to learn how to live together. The vast majority of civilians, decided not to get into trouble, kept their distances and showed an indifference tinged with distrust of the occupiers.

But with the requisition of rooms to house the troops, they finally shared a form of intimacy and cordial or simply human relationships were installed: "I was housed with a couple who had a very pretty girl. [...] One beautiful morning I wanted to leave my room for take up my service, the girl leaned against the door. I [...] on my side bent myself strongly against the door, so much so that our opposing pressures eventually raised it from its hinges, so that we were strolling through the room carrying it. All of a sudden, the partition fell and the beauty appeared in Eve's costume, to our common embarrassment and the great hilarity of her mother." (*Orages d'acier*, Ernst Jünger).

✦ German soldiers with women from the invaded territories.
The Historial de la Grande Guerre in Peronne © Yazid Medmoun.

Rarer still "pactient avec le diable" (pact with the devil), the behaviour of some women scandalised the community. In Péronne, Pierre Malicet evoked it with humour: "A midwife says there will be a lot of little Germans in Peronne next summer because females, undoubtedly for the patriotic purpose of tiring the soldiers, willingly gave them their favours". (*Le Journal de guerre de Pierre Malicet – Un magistrat des territoires occupés pendant la première guerre mondiale*, Pierre Malicet – A magistrate of the occupied territories during first World War).

If the debauchery of some was proven, genuine love stories were inevitably born from this promiscuity, romances that induce just as much sadness. After the war, when fear of occupation disappeared, these women crystallised the resentment of their fellow citizens and pay a heavy price for their "misconduct". "In certain areas, we saw damaged houses. Those were the homes of the women who had had guilty and shameful relations with the enemy . [...] Some were covered with spit from head to toes [...]. In certain areas, these demonstrations were so tumultuous that the police had to intervene and take care of punishing the guilty ones, who, for the most part had their hair cut." (Marie Masquelier, Lille, October 1918, quoted in *La France occupée 1914-1918*, Philippe Nivet).

✦ Market day at Saint Quetin, Aisne, *Gazette des Ardennes illustrée*, 16 November 1916.
The Historial de la Grande Guerre in Peronne.

✦ Women employed to do farming work by the occupation, Tertry, Somme, 1917. *The Historial de la Grande Guerre in Peronne © Yazid Medmoun.*

FORCED LABOUR AND DEPORTATIONS

After massive mobilisation in the summer of 1914, Germany recalled more than seven hundred thousand front-line workers to maintain the activity of its industry. The quota remained insufficient and Germany – although it had signed the Hague Convention in 1907 stipulating that "no civilian can be used against the effort of his own homeland" – was forced to recruit labour from the invaded territories populations. An appeal was launched but, despite an attractive salary, volunteers for a departure to Germany were rare. The failure of volunteering soon gave way to forced labour and the German army proceeded to requisition firstly male labour then female. In Belgium and Northern France, women and girls were forced to work for the enemy. "Saturday, 15 June 1918. The Germans distributed pamphlets to small girls from 12 to 15 years old. They were requested to come to work to harvest chamomile flowers, to pick nettles, etc." (*Mon Journal sous l'Occupation dans ma maison occupée par l'ennemi*, Jeanne Lefebvre).

In order to ensure the good cooperation of these civilian workers, an order by General von Armin warned the poplulation on 11 April 1917 that "The refusal to work will be punished with a penalty of imprisonment up to three years and a fine of up

✦ Notice from the *Kommandantur*, "Easy gain within the reach of everybody". By proposing to buy from the civilians fruit stones and dried nettles, the occupant showed how much Germany suffered serious shortage of raw material. The fruit stones made it possible to produce oil (from the kernel) and "coal" for the filter of the gas masks. The nettle's stems, like flax, were used in the textile industry.
The Historial de la Grande Guerre in Peronne.

to 10,000 marks". In Easter 1916, around twenty thousand women of the Lille region were deported to the rear of the Front Line to serve as a workforce in fields and factories. While the battle of Verdun raged, the situation in Germany worsened. German women strongly criticised the imperial regime that led them to famine while the military fed the populations of the invaded territories. In turn, Lille paid for this wave of dissatisfaction. By deporting these women, the military proved that enemy civilians were suffering even more and it echoes the statement of the journalist and feminist Jane Mism in an article in *La Française* (the French woman) on 19 December 1914: "As long as the war lasts, the women of the enemy will be also the enemy." In the end, the operation resembled that of a propaganda operation to appease the tensions in Germany. Public opinion among allies and among neutrals turn against them (The newspaper *La Baïonnette* published an edition entitled *Les Bourreaux de Lille* - The Lille executioners) and these women were repatriated in the following months.

✦ "The Lille executioners", *La Baïonnette*, N°.62, 7 September 1916. The Historial de la Grande Guerre in Peronne.

✦ Women requisitioned to sweep the village streets.
The Historial de la Grande Guerre in Peronne © Yazid Medmoun.

RESISTANCE AND SPYING

In Belgium and Northern France, if the majority of civilians resign themselves to the constraints of the Occupation, others were actively committed to the fight against the enemy. Resistance and espionage were organised. In this area too, women were showing their advantages by proving determination, courage and skill. Generally recruited by the secret services, they received quick training before being "released" in the field.

Taking advantage of their proximity to the enemy, they were responsible for registering the regiments present, movements of troops and equipment for organising the escape routes... From 1915 to 1918, they were dozens of networks – of which, for some, more than 50% were women – who work in the shadows and rendered invaluable services to their country.

EDITH CAVELL (1865-1915)

✦ Edith Cavell.
Wikimedia Commons.

An English nurse running the Red Cross hospital in Brussels in 1914, Edith Cavell worked with the war wounded. Joining the Louise Thuliez network, she put her energy into organising an escape route for these wounded to Holland. Arrested by the Germans on 5 August 1915, she was, after bravely acknowledging the facts, sentenced to death for espionage and shot on 12 October 1915. Her death aroused indignation around the world and ally propaganda found an additional opportunity to denounce German barbarism. Several monuments commemorate her memory (Brussels, London, Norwich ...). A future star of music, born on 19 December of the same year, was named Edith. Edith Piaf. Coincidence or, as some say, a tribute to Miss Cavell?

✦ Photograph published in *Lectures pour tous*, 1915. The execution of Edith Cavell was exploited by the recruiting sergeants (here, her portrait is presented to the crowd) to urge the young British to enlist in the army to chastise the culprits. The Historial de la Grande Guerre in Peronne.

LOUISE DE BETTIGNIES (1880-1918)

✦ Louise de Bettignies.
Wikimedia Commons.

Housekeeper in Germany before the war, Louise de Bettignies was recruited by the British secret services and used her dominance of the German language to gather information concerning the occupied troops. At the head of the Ramble network (composed of about sixty people), Louise de Bettignies – operating under the name of Alice Dubois – provided valuable information to the British: movements, staff, installations, enemy projects. She personally crossed the border fifteen times in eight months and sent men and mail between the occupied zone and England via the Netherlands. Just one month after her friend Marie-Léonie Vanhoutte, Louise de Bettignies was arrested on 20 October 1915. Sentenced to death on 16 March 1916 for espionage activities, she saw her sentence changed to fifteen years of forced labour in Germany. Interned in Siegburg camp near Cologne, she died as a result of a pleural abscess on 27 September 1918, just days before the beginning of armistice. The so-called "Joan of Arc of the North" posthumously received the cross of the Legion of Honour, the 14-18 War Cross, the British Military Medal and was made an officer of the order of the British Empire.

EMILIENNE MOREAU (1898-1971)

In February 1915, seeing the children of Loos-en-Gohelle left to fend for themselves, Émilienne Moreau improvised a school in a cellar and herself took the class. She received the authorisation of the German authorities to gather coal waste to feed the stove in her classroom and took advantage of these outings to observe the German position. On 25 September 1915, the British launched an attack to take back the village. Émilienne Moreau joined them and provided them with valuable information concerning the enemy. She participated herself in the fighting and killed several German soldiers with grenades. Her courage earned her the nickname "Loos heroine" and in one of the newspapers, *Le Petit Parisien* her memories were published in December 1915 which began with these few words: "Who would have told me, at the end of July 1914, a young girl of 16 years, I would be thrown into great adventure, and that I would play my role in the great drama of war!" Émilienne Moreau proved her courage once again during the Second World War by engaging in the Resistance and received the Companion Cross of the liberation on 11 August 1945.

Cinquième année. — N° 105.　　Le Numéro : **25** centimes.　　DIMANCHE 28 Novembre 1915.

LE MIROIR

PUBLICATION HEBDOMADAIRE, 18, Rue d'Enghien, PARIS

LE MIROIR paie n'importe quel prix les documents photographiques relatifs à la guerre, présentant un intérêt particulier.

Mlle EMILIENNE MOREAU, L'HÉROÏNE DE LOOS, CITÉE A L'ORDRE DE L'ARMÉE

✦ Emilienne Moreau on the front page of *Le Miroir*, 28 November 1915. The Historial de la Grande Guerre in Peronne.

✦ Emilienne Moreau at the age of 17 on the day of her decoration of the "Croix de Guerre" (14-18 War Cross), on 27 November 1915, at Versailles, *Le Monde illustré*, 14 December 1915. The Historial de la Grande Guerre in Peronne.

WOMEN SOLDIERS

Like Émilienne Moreau, others women were ready to take up weapons to defend their country: "Forgive me if I allow myself to write to you, but it is my French heart which dictates. So could you not also create women's regiments for the defense of our Dear Country? [...] Ah! What pride for me if you deign to accept me among all those brave.. [...] What good are women if they can not even defend their Mother Homeland, this dear France that all his children love? [...]" (Letter to the Minister of War, 27 August 1914, Marie-Louise Thomassin).

Already reluctant to see women approach the Front Lines, the French army categorically opposed seeing them endorse the uniform and will keep this line of conduct for the duration of the conflict.

✦ British uniform for the Women's Auxiliary Corps.
The Historial de la Grande Guerre in Peronne © Yazid Medmoun.

✦ Marie Marvingt, 1910 .
The Library of Congress USA.

MARIE MARVINGT (1875-1963)

Marie Marvingt was a pioneer in many areas. Before the war, she passed her driving license and, passionate about aeronautics, her pilot's license; she practiced many sports such as cycling, mountaineering, fencing... Of course, when the war broke out in 1914, the one that was called "the fiancee of danger" or "Marie Daredevil" wanted to take part in the adventure. Under a masculine identity and dressed as a man, we find her with the "Poilus" on the Front Line; quickly unmasked she was still allowed to stay on the Front as a nurse. Using her experience as a pilot she proposed to organise the transport of wounded by plane and took part in the first bombing operations. The "Croix de la Guerre" (War Cross) was awarded to her in 1915 after the attack on a German barracks of Metz. She was made knight of the Legion of Honour in 1935.

✦ Marie Marvignt in the French Blue Horizon uniform. Intercontinentale, AFP.

In Britain, women had the opportunity to fulfill their "military duty" by engaging in the spring of 1917 in the Women's Army Auxiliary Corps. The goal of the WAAC was to assign to military headquarters a women's unit able to make themselves useful, allowing the male workforce to fully dedicate themselves to the armed service. It was about making their actions complementary: men in the line of fire, women in the services at the rear. More than 40,000 women enlist in the WAAC during the war: wearing the uniform, subjected to discipline and military laws, they provided many jobs and were recognized "Soldiers" in their own right. Only Russia took one step further following the revolution of February 1917 and created female battalions. The goal was to show the soldiers who were balking to continue the fight that the women were ready. So it was about touching man's pride to remobilise them. It is estimated that five thousand women served in these seventeen battalions (only two of them will be deployed on the Front). From August 1917, the army distanced itself from the female battalions and the first were dismantled in September. But some of these fighters showed their determination by being among the last to defend the Winter Palace against the Bolsheviks in the night of 25-26 October 1917.

MARIA BOTCHKAREVA (1889-1920)

As a simple peasant, Maria Botchkareva joined, as early as 1914, the 25th Tomsk Reserve Battalion with a personal derogation from the Tsar. While revolutionary unrest shuck Russia in March 1917 she received authorisation from the Provisional Government to form a female battalion of which she took the command. After intensive training, the "death battalion" was sent to the front; the losses were high and Maria Botchkareva, nicknamed Yashka, was herself seriously hurt. At the fall of the Provisional Government, threatened by Bolsheviks, she took refuge in the United States. She returned to her homeland in August 1918 and formed a nursing unit integrated with the Red Cross. Arrested by the Cheka and declared an enemy of the people, She was shot on 15 May 1920.

✦ Maria Botchkareva during her exile in the United States in 1918. The Library of Congress USA.

✦ The "Dealth Battalion" in training: "They despise death and fear only to be made prisoners: they were provided with a dose of cyanide that should be absorb if they were captured", *Le Monde illustré*, 25 August 1917.
The Historial de la Grande Guerre in Peronne.

WOMEN AND THE OUTCOME OF WAR

WIDOWS

✦ Poster for a charity concert given for the benefit of the mutilated and widows of war. The Historial de la Grande Guerre in Peronne © Yazid Medmoun.

In consequence of the extreme loss of life on the battlefields, France had more than six hundred and thirty thousand widows in late 1918 (about three million in the world). Omnipresent in the landscape of the time, the black silhouettes symbolised the trauma experienced and the bereavement of the nation. Deprived of the head of the family, for many their employment lost, numerous widows understood insecurity. As during the war, solidarity took over and the Charities organised various actions in their favour (concerts, galas, exhibitions, raffles...). Aware of these difficulties, the State reserved jobs in the public service for widows and the law of 31 March 1919 entitled them to a pension. However, the payment of the said pension ended when the woman remarried; the legislature intended to dissuade Widows from "taking a man" from the young girls of age to marry (this did not prevent more than 40% of them from remarrying once the ten-month period of mourning had elapsed). In 1921, because of the lack of men or loyalty to commitment made to a fiance before leaving, 13% of young girls, the "white widows", stayed single. "There was a shortage of young people and those who were still virgins can keep their virginity, unless they are content with one the many cripples who have lost an arm or a leg." (Léon Pénet, letter to his wife, quoted in *Paroles de Poilus, Lettres et carnets du front 1914-1918*, Jean-Pierre and Yves Laplume).

✦ Ceremonial plate: "To my husband. My heart, from your thought, is nourished every day. We are separated but I still love you." The Historial de la Grande Guerre in Peronne © Yazid Medmoun.

✦ Widowers in the streets of Bovelles, Somme. The Historial de la Grande Guerre in Peronne © Yazid Medmoun.

Even before their return from the Front, men wondered about their reintegration into a society that had evolved without them, a society where women had asserted themselves: "Winning income [the soldier] would he suffer from finding a home deserted, where his so dearly claimed authority would be recognized no more? [...] Would anyone tell him on his return that socially there was no more, men and women, but two equal beings in law, two social units? Fallen from his age-old role of protector just when he had, once again, deserved this title, would he accept to share with women the civil and political struggles? To find her as a rival everywhere, competitor to the jobs he aspires, and where she has already taken a serious advance? [...]." (Trench Journal *L'Horizon*, December 1918, quoted in *14-18, Les Combattants des tranchées*, Stéphane Audoin-Rouzeau).

✦ Poster "The peace loan" by Henri Lebasque, 1920. With peace, the pre-war social codes are redeemed: the man works, the woman nourishes.
The Historial de la Grande Guerre in Peronne © Yazid Medmoun.

✦ Bronze statue by Alexandre Descatoire, "The return of the soldier".
The Historial de la Grande Guerre in Peronne © Yazid Medmoun.

Upon the signing of the armistice, the Ministry of Reconstruction was quick to reassure them by a circular of 13 November 1918 recalling women to their duty: "By returning to your old occupations or taking on other work during this time of peace, you will be useful to your country, as you have dedicated yourself for four years to the work of war". This decision for the less expeditious seemed to close bluntly the parenthesis of the war: women were "invited" to return and focus on their secular role. As well as, to encourage their departure, Minister Louis Loucheur promised a bonus corresponding to one months salary to all workers of the armament who vacated their positions by 5 December 1918. The preoccupation of the moment, before any other consideration was to allow the demobilised combatants to regain a foothold in the work market. This was the price for the happiness caused by the return of the spouse.

At the same time, the frightful decline in population pushed the state to make the birthrate a national priority. The law of 31 July 1920 clearly affirmed this expectation and repressed severely "provocation to abortion and contraceptive propaganda". Women were encouraged to procreate and so, to demonstrate an entirely different way of their "Patriotism". France returned to its pre-war concerns when, worried about the German demographic superiority, incited its women to have children. By asking women to be mothers, was also an opportunity to return to traditional values.

If the return of the men upset the social universe of four years of war, cohabitation was no longer a simple formality. How to resume life where it had been left, as if nothing had happened? "What are we going to do with them? guys who are only good at fighting? [...] Ask the Corps, to adapt to the salad? He was trained to hunt and the hunt is finished. He will pluck him to the death if he plucks a hen... [...] Suppose there are [men] who are frank enough to confess, I do not say they don't regret, but they have lived only that... Will they have to hide it like a chancre. And yet, they did not ask to go!... And then, all their provisions of nerve, they no longer have any use. It will stifle them. They will die of congestion..." (*Captain Conan*, Roger Vercel).

Men, of course, had changed. The women as well. Everyone had a new experience without having shared it with the other. After being "out of sight" during the war, they must relearn to know each other and to live with a new sharing of authority and responsibilities. Some couples found themselves happily. Others struggled more when men were haunted by war and became taciturn, felt misunderstood and closed up in a heavy silence, tried to forget and took refuge in alcohol...

Each couple was simply trying to rebuild and it was futile to hope to conclude globally. But the evolution in the number divorces (34,079 in 1920 – mainly asked by men, marked a reversal of pre-war codes – against 16,330 in 1913) reveals how difficult it was to escape unscathed from this war.

✦ Poster by the League for the raise in the French birth rate and for the defense of large families, "It's not enough to cry "Vive la France!" We must make it live", 1920. On the map of France in the background, mortality is higher than the birth rate in the departments marked in black.
The Historial de la Grande Guerre in Peronne © Yazid Medmoun.

✦ Poster by the French women's union against alcohol.
The Historial de la Grande Guerre in Peronne © Yazid Medmoun.

CONCLUSION

The Great War was not the only a men's affair. The constraints it imposed to society, the sacrifices and the efforts it asked of everyone, upset the landmarks which had governed for so long. Women were called to play a major role and proved that they were capable to do as much and as well as the men, gone to fight. Their commitment was recognised throughout these four years of war but at the signing of the armistice, only the soldier, heroic defender of the homeland, received the tribute of the nation. Forgotten in the celebration of the "Victory", some women – and "munitionnettes" that received the best wages are the main targets – are seen considered by some to be "profiteers of war". After so much effort, after demonstrating their abilities, women were certainly allowed to have the right to hope that some of their pre-war claims (put on hold during the Sacred Union from August 1914) would be considered. The reality was different. The "new" wife failed to impose herself in the post-war society that only aspires to a return to traditional values where the woman was above all a wife, good mistress of the house and devoted mother. Their legal status remained the one that d e f i n e d   the Civil Code of 1804 Article 213 which clearly states that "the husband must protect his wife, the woman owes obedience to her husband" (the incapacity was lifted by the law of 18 February 1938). The question of the right to vote, obtained by the Germans and the English from 1918 and constituting one of the main claims of French women, remains unanswered until 1922 where the Senate, although the National Assembly declared to be favourable, opposed it (this refusal was reiterated in 1932 and the right to vote, so much hoped for was only granted with the ordinance of 22 April 1944). The idea that the emancipation of women took place during the First World War should be taken with care. If it is undeniable

✦ Patriotic plate paying tribute to "The valiant and graceful women of France, never tiring, never cowardly". The Historial de la Grande Guerre in Peronne © Yazid Medmoun.

that inequalities were dwindling, they remained socially present, economically and legally.

Anyway, and despite the conservative will of a part of society, an irreversible process had been set in motion and undeniable advances materialised: better access to certain jobs in the tertiary sector, the right to start their own businesses (even if the right to practice a profession without the authorisation of their husband was only granted by the law of 13 July 1965), the right to open a bank account, opening of some schools to girls allowing them to engage in higher studies and pass the baccalaureate... The women therefore acquired rights. Also, individual freedom as the picture of the "boy" – of which Coco Chanel was one instigators – which shook up the codes of fashion: corsets, long dresses and buns gave way to trousers (already obliged to be worn in some of the war factories), skirts shorter and more masculine hairstyles. The place and the image of the woman had evolved and the woman of the "Roaring Twenties" (1920-1929) was no longer that of the "Belle Epoque" (late 19th century-1913). How could it be? How could it be possible to draw a line on the years of war and to act as if nothing had happened? It's certain, now, "nothing would be like before..."

✦ "Roaring Twenties" dress, pink silk with embroidery. The Historial de la Grande Guerre in Peronne © Yazid Medmoun.